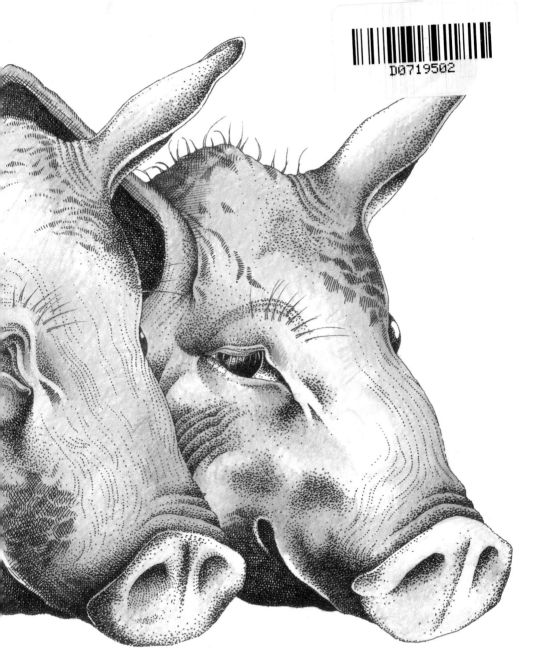

'I haven't clawed my way to the top
of the food chain just to eat vegetables.'
charles jarvis

AND SO I FACE THE
VINYL CURTAIN...

Drawings and Verses
by Simon Drew

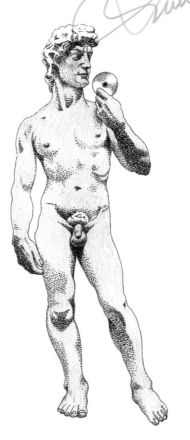

MICHELANGELO'S DVD

ANTIQUE COLLECTORS' CLUB

to Caroline

a problem shared is gossip

©2005 Simon Drew
World copyright reserved

ISBN 1 905377 01 0

British Library Cataloguing-in-Publication Data
A catalogue record for this book is available from the British Library

Printed in China
for the Antique Collectors' Club Ltd., Woodbridge, Suffolk

MOLE VAULTING

chicken in the basket

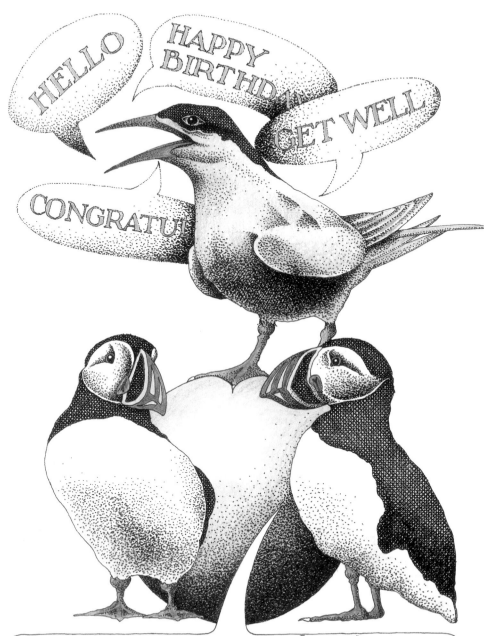

Munch's "The Scrum"

ONE PENNY

RARE
BEEF

ME
BE

DIUM
EF

WELL
DONE
BEEF

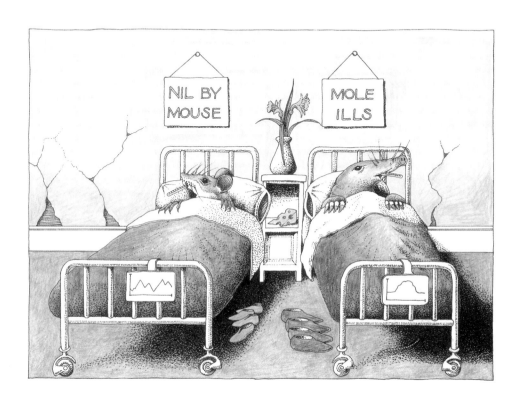

THE GARAGE OF FIGARO

also known as: car men

See the mothers in the park:
they're rather ugly, chiefly.
Someone must have loved them once
but in the dark, and briefly.

Your call is very important to us
but all our opera haters are
busy at the moment

the aardvark of liberty

FISH C

CAKES

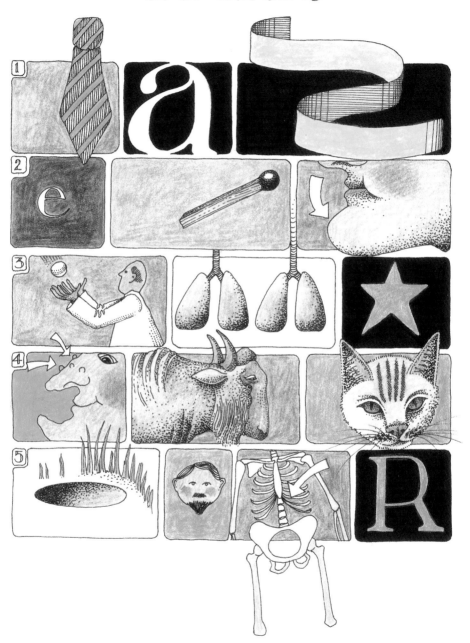

SPOT THE SONG

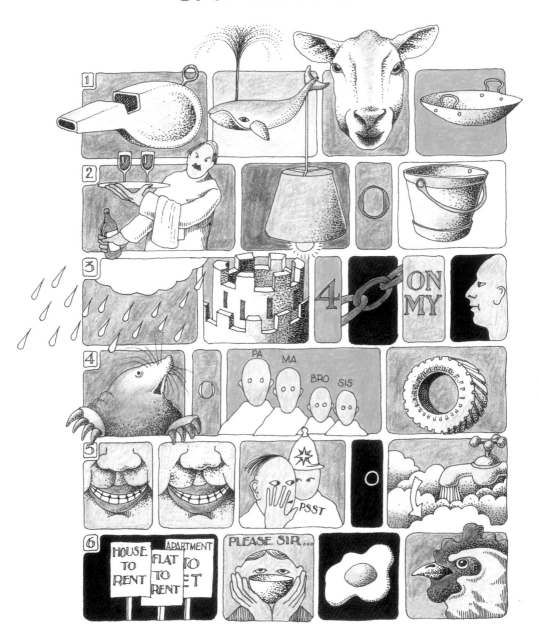

SPOT THE NURSERY RHYME

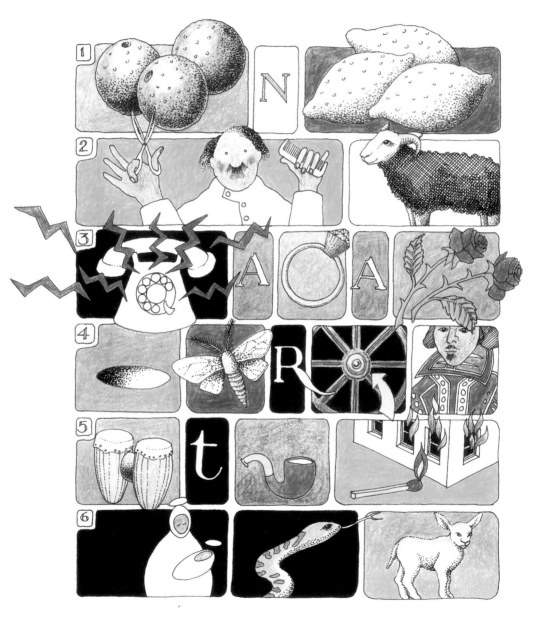

mole in one

Elgin's cat playing with his marbles

important vegetables in history:

king edward
the sixth

All around us dangers wait,
worse than any thriller:
somewhere hidden in a field
there lurks a cereal killer.

..... suddenly, in a cave, they
discovered the dead sea squirrels.

hell's angler

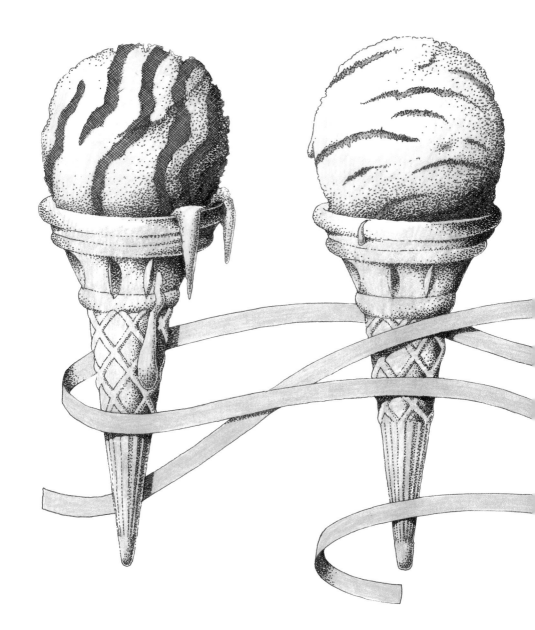

STILL LIFE WITH

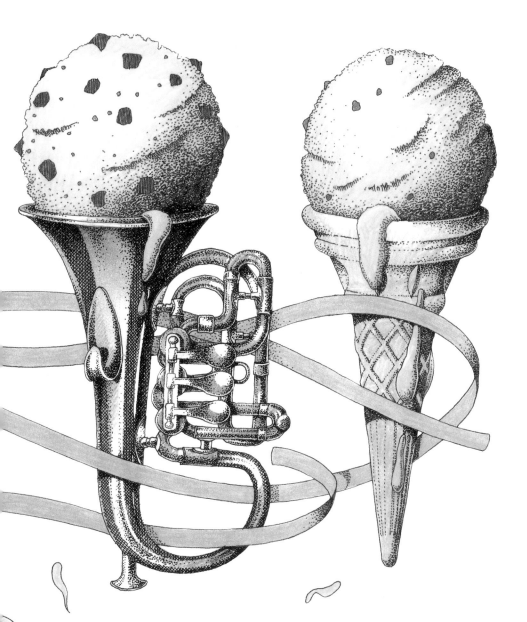

CORNETS......

sponge
victoria

black
doris
gateau

graham
brulée

queen of
puddings

DESSER

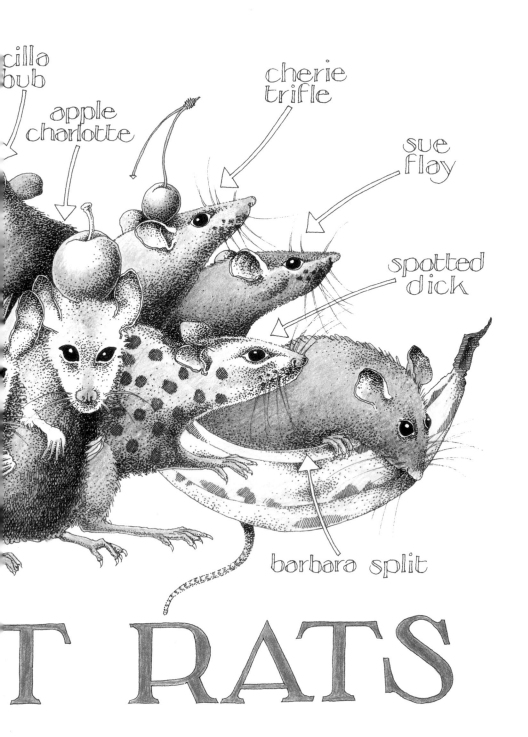

cilla
bub

apple
charlotte

cherie
trifle

sue
flay

spotted
dick

barbara split

T RATS

the lit-mouse test

flute salad
(with a little duck)

If I had all the money I've spent on drink, I'd spend it on drink.

vivian stanshall

wedding ring

HORNITHOLOGY

SALVADOR deli

WIMBLEDOG

CAPTAIN COOK

DINER

SAURS

deaf in venice

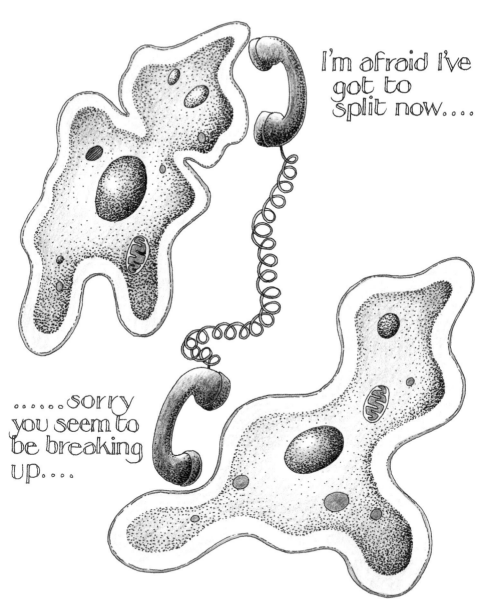

CELL PHONES

fried scrambled
 coddled

FREE R

scotch benedict pooched

RANGE

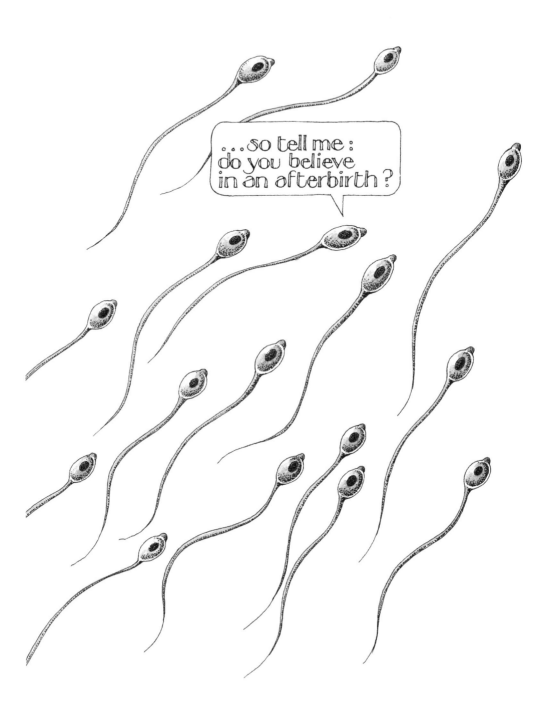

baby on board

mask a pony